Forty Games for Frivolous People

40 GAMES FOR FRIVOLOUS PEOPLE

BY PETER WILSON

DRAWINGS BY CONNY JUDE

quick fox

New York ○ London ○ Tokyo

CONTENTS

Consequences (*contd*)

WHAT TO PLAY WHEN

 sedate

 alcohol helps

 not to be attempted unless befuddled by alcohol

 time everyone went home

 pencil and paper

 physical contact

 grounds for divorce

 good car game

 not under any circumstances to be attempted in the car

 rowdy

 likely to result in neighbours banging on the walls

 likely to induce sobbing and failure of self-confidence

To Elspeth
and Richard

INTRODUCTION

The aim of this book is to provide some ideas to follow that moment (whether euphoric or desperate) when somebody cries 'Let's play a game!'

The choice has deliberately been limited to games which can be played around the dining table or in the sitting room with no props at all, or pencils and paper at most. No-one wants to spend half the evening searching for seven packs of cards, two walking sticks and a pineapple. (One or two games, like Newspaper Taxis, don't really belong here on this basis but they are too good to exclude.) I do know some other games, and those readers who wish to learn about them should write to me enclosing a stamped, addressed envelope, a photograph, and a signed letter of permission from a bishop.

The book is short relative to most others of its type. I felt when I was doing my scouting around that too many games can be bewildering rather than amusing, like a hall full of distorting mirrors all shrieking for attention. What can you do but wander around with your mouth open? Further, compilers of such vast catalogues cannot possibly have played every game themselves, and the describing of them becomes mechanical.

That's why I have limited the number of games in this book to forty.

iii BONUS !!!

Numerate readers will notice that there are *more than forty*.

There are one or two points to be made before the fun starts. This book does not try to cover ground already mapped by Stephen Potter: local advantage and bullying. Don't forget: if they're in your house then they'll play by your rules. Since rules are as various as dialects, settling clearly exactly which ones you are going to use will save trouble later. This applies especially to Charades, which is a sort of lingua franca of true games players, but the particular brand of Charades that you know may bear only a flickering resemblance to anyone else's. Get your oar in FIRST.

Losers or players eliminated in early rounds may be subjected to some suitably humiliating forfeit. Some old favourites are

Getting down on all fours and making a noise like a donkey.

Going to the nearest bedroom and putting on the first garment your hand touches in the first drawer down.

Crawling through the paddlewheel—that is, through the legs of the other players as they paddle the retreating rump.

Drinking a 'window' of a pint or other drink (but if you are trying these games in the snug bar of the Dog and Loofah you might find yourselves startled and blinking on the High Street before you get round to the forfeits).

Losing, like winning, is not everything although in some moods you may think that there is nothing else. What is everything to a game is how much fun it is, whether it is a sedentary form of croquet, brain-washing or burning at the stake. Much depends on the mood of a party, and for this reason the games are marked with appropriate symbols. The most valuable lesson you can learn is

'Win, lose,

Home's best'.

No offence is intended by referring to players throughout as 'he'. It's just easier not to have to go through 'He/she then puts the tube between his/her knees and blows . . .' the dozens of times it would be necessary. I tossed a coin to decide if *he* or *she* was to stand for *you*, and *he* won.

My thanks go to my editor, to Conny Jude for her anarchic illustrations and to KAG for the jacket photograph. Advertisements flushed out a number of games new to me, and their beaters are credited in the text.

PW

BOTTICELLI

A 'Let's play Botticelli!'
Omnes 'Ooh! Yes! Let's! Coo-ee!'

Player A starts by thinking of a figure—real or fictional—of whom the others might reasonably have heard. (Pete Wycza, a patrolman in Donald E. Westlake's *Killing Time* doesn't qualify, and neither do fifteenth century monks who write treatises on East Anglian orthography. Or even *in* E.A. orthography.)

A gives the others the initial letter of the name he is harbouring.

Joan of Arc starts with J, not A, and Henry V with H not F. Best to establish ground rules in advance, or you may have some Awful Scenes (sobbing in the bathroom, that sort of thing).

The other players first ask A indirect questions to identify characters *they* think up, whose initials are the same as the one given. If the chosen initial is B, the dialogue might run as follows:

B Are you a witty Oxford don?
A No. I am not Maurice Bowra.
C Are you the Editor of the Washington Post?
A No. I am not Ben Bradlee.
D Are you a poet sometimes eaten with meat?
A Give up.
D Browning.

D now gets to ask a direct question about whoever A has in mind.

D Are you real or fictional?

A must answer truthfully. In most versions A may only answer Yes or No to direct questions, and D's direct question would be wasted, but where alternatives are given the effect is the same. After all, if the Mystery Person is not real, what else could he/she be? (rhetorical question).

The game continues. Each time A cannot identify the name thought of by a questioner, he must answer a direct question. Direct questions follow an epically formulaic pattern:

1. Are you real or fictional?
2. Male or female?
3. If real, are you alive today? If fictional, are you in a book written before 1900?
4. The next stage is to fix the character's dates more precisely—for instance which side of 1600 did he flourish?
5. What is the character famous for? If real, was he a scientist/novelist/politician or what? If fictional, from a book/play/opera/public service message/comic strip?

There is a particularly testing form of Botticelli in which the questioners—trying hard to outwit the man in the middle—must limit their questions to conform to the information already elicited from preceding direct questions.

Thus, if it is established that the mystery person is female, dead, and flourished in the nineteenth century, and began with B, then all the indirect questions *must* refer to women with exactly those attributes.

Don't worry. There are only three Brontës and one Elizabeth Barrett Browning. Thank goodness.

ZIP

A simple and entertaining vocabulary game, in which the object is to identify words from their initial letters, parts of speech, and dictionary definitions. You will, naturally enough, need a dictionary at hand. One person opens the dictionary and reads out at random, say,

'M. Noun. General slaughter of unresisting persons'.

The first person who thinks he's got it says Zip! (Those of you who guessed that this is where the title comes from get to choose the next eight forfeits.)
If the guess is wrong, score −1
If the guess is right, score +2
First person to 10 takes over the dictionary. The object is to make one's own turn with the dictionary last as long as possible. The beginner might therefore want to search for obscure technical words. This is a mistake, as it only leads to the wrong sort of frustrations and may result in an example of what is defined above. The canny questioner will pick on words—and there is usually a fair choice on each page—that are irritatingly familiar and surrounded by synonyms, for instance

'H. Noun. Place, gap, opening, cavity.'

The competitors have the choice of 'hole' or 'hollow' and I would let them turn in the wind.

4

SQUARE WHOLE

Each player squares off a piece of paper, exactly matching the number of horizontal and vertical squares to the number of players. Each player chooses a category and a letter. The topic is put on the horizontal, the letter on the vertical. If you have any argument about this the crowd you're playing with probably isn't the right type and you'd better reshuffle your friends. So the grid might look like this

	BIRDS	FLOWERS	COLOURS	TURKISH NOVELISTS
R				
S				
B				
X				

1. Each player has chosen a category that presumably suits him. This is *wise*.

2. The first three are clearly out to win.

3. The fourth is out to wreck. Show him the door or the booze.

4. Each square corresponds to a different category/initial letter combination. It is each player's job to get as many words as possible into each square.

5. A time limit is set, usually three minutes. During this time silence is observed.

Scoring as follows, if you're into that kind of thing. Marks are weighted towards originality. If, for example, under Musical Comedy Characters you have Papageno and Papagena as well as Pooh-Bah, you ought to score more than the moron who forgot Papageno. (Correspondence will not be entered into as to the position of *The Magic Flute* in the canon of world music. I don't care if you find it moving, tragic or Rosicrucian. If the Papageni are meant to be funny they're comedy.)

1 point for an entry duplicated by all the other players.

2 points for a duplication by all but one.

3 points for a duplication by all but two.

4 points for a duplication by all but three, and so on.

The maximum score for any entry—if no-one else has it—is the same as the number of people playing. Isn't the universe *logical*?

FOUR-LETTER WORDS

This is a verbal form of the board game in which players try to discover their opponent's arrangement of coloured pegs by progressive elimination of other arrangements.

All players choose four-letter key words, and write them down, but *without letting other players see them*. This is to forestall cheating by changing the word in mid-game, which does happen in some circles.

Let us say that A's key word is TEAM. B, on A's right, must try to find out what A's word is by supplying A with a series of guess words. A must respond with how many letters in the guess word correspond to letters in the key word. At the same time, C is trying to find out what B's word is, and so on round the table. With luck on B's side, the exchanges might go like this

B   FOXY?
A   None.
B   BITS?
A   One.
B   EMIT?
A   Three.
So B now knows that the word contains T, E and M.
B   MATE?
A   Four.

All B has to do now is hit upon the right arrangement of the letters. A has been clever, as he usually is. He has picked four letters that add up to a number of different words, and it may take B several guesses before he happens on the right one. Meanwhile A may well crack G's word to win the game.

Complications arise when A chooses a key word that has a double or a treble letter in it. The response to each guess word must reflect how many letters have been scored out of the total four, including duplications. Say the key word is LOLL and the guess word is TILT. A would respond 'Three', and it would be up to B to discover whether it is three different letters, two the same or three the same. So remember to test for duplicated letters at some stage.

FILLET

A word is chosen at random, of as many letters as the company desires.

It is written up and down again in two columns, thus:

D	Y
E	R
S	O
U	T
L	L
T	U
O	S
R	E
Y	D

by each player.

Silence is then enforced for an agreed period of time.

(A   Three minutes?

B   Fine

C   Fine

D   Can we make it four?

A   Fine

B   Fine

C   Fine

E   What about the babysitter darling?

D   What about her, sweetheart?

E   She's waiting for us

D   Hum

C   Three will do fine for me, honestly.

A little democracy can sometimes not be a help.

They'll have three and like it.)

Each player, in the silent period, fills in each line with the longest word he can think of, provided it begins and ends with the right letters. When the time is up, players compare words. Unique words count one for each syllable; duplications are eliminated.

The game finishes when the first player reaches an agreed total of points. He is then given a cabin cruiser and a holiday in the Virgin Islands.

Film Stars

This is a down-market version of Fillet, very popular with children and younger brothers who know the name of every single football player *ever*. Like selecting the Biblical XI to meet the Beautiful People XI, it is a marvellous game for when you are BORED. Just write the alphabet out vertically in the right hand column, and on the left as much of any old well-known phrase or saying as will fit. Choose

STAR CARDS

Elvis

a category, then fill in names whose initials are given by the two columns, thus:

I	A
T	B
Ian	Carmichael
Sammy	Davis Jr.
A	E
Fred	Flintstone
A	G
Robert	Hope
F	I
A	J
R	K
B	L
Ethel	Merman
T	N
T	O
Elvis	Presley
R	Q
T	R
Harry	Secombe
I	T
N	U
G	V
Tammy	Wynette
H	X
A	Y
T	Z

A time limit of five minutes or so is usually imposed. Score 2 points for names which no-one else has and 1 point for duplicates. The category above is Famous Entertainers and Film Stars. On wet afternoons in the clubhouse the subject could

just as well be Famous Golfers, Cricketers, Sports-
people; for children drop the category and make it
just Anyone Famous; and for those long, boring
civil rights cases at the Law Courts, why not have a
go with Famous Courtesans?

CAN I COME WITH YOU?

A   I am going to Papua New Guinea, and I will take a bottle but not a top.

B   Ah. If I take a table but not a cloth, can I come with you?

A   No.

Le silence éternel de ces espaces tombe comme une brique. Enfin:

C   If I take a kettle but not a cup, can I come with you?

A   I should be honoured.

The point is, and C has spotted it, that A's criterion for selecting his baggage is that items must have double letters in them. Let's have another go:

A   I am going to Swindon ...

B   Bad luck.

C   ... and I will take a cow but not a dog.

B   If I take a pig but not a cat, can I come with you?

A   Nope.

B performs a forfeit and is taken out to be buried.

C   If I take the Ram Jam Band but not the London String Players, can I come with you?

A   Yes.

Clever old C has got it again. A only wants horns along on this trip. The game gets more outlandish as people get used to it.

You might find the following categories useful to begin with: double vowels, one particular vowel, more than one vowel, hyphenations, endings in a particular letter, only animals whose names are also anagrams, only root vegetables . . .

IN COMMON

A game for the quick-witted. The rest of you can play with your building blocks.

A   What have the following in common?
     Oh! Calcutta!, BBC sports coverage, and London Transport.
B   Dunno.
A   Aha! Three men called Kenneth: Kenneth Tynan, Kenneth Wostenholme and Kenneth Robinson. Your turn.
B   Ermmmmmmmmmmmmm.
     What have the following in common?
     Danny La Rue, Sean Connery, Reginald Bosanquet.
A   Hairpieces.
B   Jolly good.
A   What have the following in common?
     Oxford, New York and Bach.
B   Sir, I cannot tell.
A   St John's College, Oxford; the Cathedral of St John, New York; and the St John Passion by Bach.
B   Sir, I wonder at your connexion.
A   Sir, I wonder at it myself. Where's the coffee?

The game goes on until it stops; that's its delight. It is possible to go on for hours, becoming more and more obscure. Connexions between people and objects may be as outrageous as you like, so long as their obscurity doesn't produce unfair baffling.

17

Thus

A   What have the following in common?
     Mendeleev, the Lone Ranger and Ian Fleming.

B   (yawning) No idea.

A   Mendeleev was the father of the Periodic Table
     of the Elements, the Lone Ranger's horse was
     called Silver (an element) and Ian Fleming
     wrote *Goldfinger*, also an element.

B   Does anyone want a lift home?

Keep it tricky, witty and clear and the connexions
can be a delight to unravel, making the game as
much fun as, say, Botticelli.

BUILD A HOUSE

'I have heard of a man who had a mind to sell his house, and therefore carried a piece of brick in his pocket, which he shewed as a pattern to encourage purchasers'   Jonathan Swift

A number of these sedate, early-evening games have a distinctly therapeutic air to them. Certainly *Build a House* at its best depends on a degree of empathy and care which can be wholly beneficial. It can, though not strictly a game, also be a source of fun and good-natured teasing.

Each player in turn becomes the focus of the others, who describe an imaginary house they think would suit him best.

It would, of course, be logical to describe the house in order: the garden, the front door, the shape of the doormat (would it have WELCOME on it?), the pictures, the staircarpet, and on, on, to the colour of the bathroom suite . . .

Less fun if everybody actually owns a house which the others all know. Also there can be a problem if the game is played in the wrong spirit. Those whose houses are not being described might get bored and malicious, so beware of destructive elements. But perhaps these are really what fascinate in all thinly-disguised Truth Games?

From C R Patmore

19

CONCERTINA

One of a number of games in which unfair advantage is given to Scrabble players and crossword buffs. You know—the sort of people who read detective novels and try to work out for themselves who's dunnit.

The idea is to add a letter to a sequence without completing a word. Say player A begins with 'Q'; the player on his right—B—might say 'U', and indeed he would be advised to because he can be challenged at any time about the word he has in mind as he adds his letter, and he can't have many words in his quiver that begin with Q and don't continue with U. Proper names are not allowed, which rules out QANTAS.

So the sequence so far is QU. The next player might add E, the next S, and player E (for it is he) is then faced with QUES, to which he must add a letter towards a longer word without completing a shorter word. If he aims at QUESTION he will complete QUEST and have to drop out or submit to a forfeit before a new round begins.

There are two further variations on these basic rules. The first ensures that the game doesn't end too quickly and that interesting words can be embarked upon simply by stipulating that no word is complete under four letters. TEA, for instance, doesn't count, but TEAS, TEAK, TEAT, TEAM etc. all do.

In the second variation players are allowed, if they wish, to take the sequence of letters presented to them and make an anagram of it, so that the addition of one more letter makes a different almost-word.

Thus
A
AT
ATE
ASTE
SEATE
STEAME
MASTERE
and so on, if you can.

This game is more enjoyable played with opponents of roughly equal ability, and you will find that the fun to be had from forcing word-endings on to other people is almost as much as evading them yourself.

22

SUITCASES

Players are asked to imagine that they are going on holiday and are packing their suitcases. A letter of the alphabet is chosen, and only items beginning with that letter may be taken. Ten minutes allowed for players to write out their lists.

One point is scored for any unduplicated items. I ought to quote the source of this game: 'The beginner tends to concentrate on the size of his suitcase, whereas the experienced player thinks of ... a furniture van, relying on wit and persuasion when the counting up starts'.

Guidelines

Prefixes don't count within the individual player's list. He wouldn't get away with Toothpaste, -brush, -pick, -mug, etc. But from one player to the next, duplication of this sort is less rigidly stamped on. Bulky objects (the Statue of Liberty, the Sun, Samson) can be the subject of special pleading. Dinghies can be inflatable and stockings have ladders. Live animals, including fish and insects, are not encouraged, although many ducks are rubber. Extreme Bad Taste is rewarded or penalized according to the degree of wit, the whim of the players, and the level in the decanter.

From M I Oliver

THE INTERVIEW

Gorgonised me from head to foot
With a stony British stare

Lord Tennyson

Four or five players who don't know the game (my! what a *lot* of people you know) leave the room. They are asked to re-enter one by one, and to sit in the middle of the room where everybody can see them. Nothing happens. The others simply sit and stare. There is no movement or sound from anyone

but the man-in-the-middle until he actually says

'I know! You're not saying anything and hoping that it will disturb me! How frightfully clever!'
or
'Excuse me. Has anyone any pentathol?'

At this point the next contestant is asked to enter. The game continues.

Not to be played to fill out those long winter evenings, since it won't.

From Dr G D Chryssides

NAMING TOWNS

A useful test of geographical awareness.

The game is limited at the beginning to a particular category—towns in the British Isles, for example. One person throws out, say, *Six pines.*

A (always the first to
   dive in)   Six pines.
B and C in chorus   Sevenoaks!
A   Rats.
B and C (who have
      decided that the
      only way to
      beat A is to
      team up)   Cat finger.
A (nonplussed)   Felixstowe?

The clue divides up the name in any way possible and makes any possible connexion.

A (trying hard)   Frank nose.
B and C   Sidmouth.
B and C   Sprout meadow
                        seasoner pound.
A (gibbering slightly) Go on. Tell me.
B and C   Budleigh Salterton!

CHARTER

The group decides on a basic crossword grid, say:

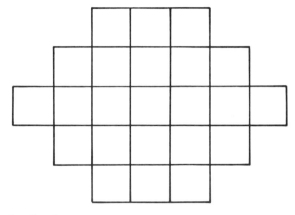

and all players take it down on their pieces of paper.

Entr'acte: Music from *Seven Brides for Seven Brothers* starring Jane Powell and Howard Keel, directed by Stanley Donen.

All finished? Good.

Starting arbitrarily, letters are called out round the table, and everyone fills in their crossword without reference to anyone else. It's like Bingo, but without the loneliness.

The object is to make as many and as long words as possible, for which rewards are given.

The contributor who suggested this game specified that letters should be pulled out of a hat or box (but, please, *not* a hatbox). This, however, since it involves the host in cutting out little bits of paper or ransacking the Scrabble set when he should be doing something rather special to the veal, can be dispensed with as overcomplicated.

Each player tries to complete his own words by calling out letters he needs when his turn comes. Each player will be frustrated by the others' choices. The same judgment that tells you when to hang on to the blank, the 'x' and two 's's in Scrabble will be required in placing each letter.

Scoring: in the grid given above, the longest possible word will contain seven letters. Maximum score with one word is therefore seven.
Score five for each five-letter word, and so on.
For example, arch gamester A's paper might be

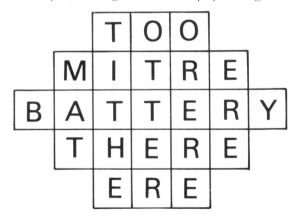

and B's paper

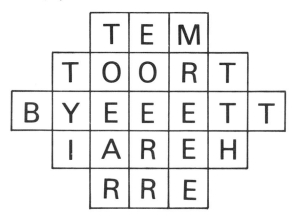

	T	E	M		
T	O	O	R	T	
B	Y	E	E	E	T	T
I	A	R	E	H	
	R	R	E		

A's score is, if you tot it all up and insist on counting 'ere' as a word notwithstanding archaism, 39.

B's score is 0.

A wins by remembering that 'e's are safest at the end of words.

Rah, rah, A.

From Dr G D Chryssides

MY FIRST IS

'All are but parts of one stupendous whole'
Alexander Pope

This is an old game used to keep people quiet: dissenting Churchmen, Welsh rugby fans, troubled philosophers and so on.

Success is not guaranteed.

The idea is to divide up a word or name—just as you might in Charades—and to present it in the wittiest possible way according to the formula 'My first is ...' Thus

A   (your old friend) My first and second are a city connected with King Lear.
My third and fourth are what water comes out of.
Yet my whole is magic on the turf.
Who am I?

B   Indeed.
Hmmmmmmmmmmmmmm ...
I give up.

A   Leicester Spigot!

It is as important to mislead on the 'whole' as on its parts. Thus Winston Churchill might be identified as a painter, Harold Hobson as a Christian Scientist, Vita Sackville-West as a gardener and Elton John as chairman of a football club.

IN MY END IS MY BEGINNING

A category is chosen by someone—anyone—the one with a J in his name—the richest—the last to sit down—oh, very well, the one with the strongest personality. He begins with a category and a name from his category, and the object is to start your word with the final letter of the previous word.

A   I'll begin. Famous Italians.

B,C,D etc exhibit symptoms of incipient rebellion.

A   Galileo.
B   Ovid.
C   Dante.
D   Erasmus.
A   Sorry.
B   That's all right.
A   No, Erasmus wasn't Italian.
D   Not even a little bit?
A   Well, not much. You'll have to drop out.
D   (sotto voce) Bully.
A   (continuing) Enrico Bearzot.
B   Tacitus.

Etc.

From R Harrison

CHARADES

The idea of charades is very simple. You must convey a message without speaking or using any props. You therefore become a mime artist, except that you're not wearing black leotards or white face makeup, and you're not being paid. Your message is given to you by your opponents in the expectation that you will humiliate yourself in trying to convey it. It is therefore called 'a nasty'.

There are several varieties of the game, one of which is

Team charades

Two teams, as near equal in numbers as possible, are chosen and then separate. Each team takes a pen and enough paper to supply each member of the opposing team with nasties twice over—twice because it's only in the second round that folk really warm to their obligation to keep the company amused.

You can choose messages from any category you like: proper names, songs, books, films, musicals, opera, plays, television programmes, well-known phrases or sayings and Shakespeare are the usual fare. Don't choose anything too obscure because it becomes a bore to perform and guess, and take care in assigning your nasties to make them as apt—or inapt—as possible for the individual recipients.

The teams gather and sit round a common acting

area. The fun lies in seeing how the members of the other team cope with your nasties, and you are allowed to distract them in any way you like as one of your opponents gamely struggles to convey the title *Whitaker's Almanack* to the other members of his team.

A toss of a coin decides which team goes first. The captain begins by collecting his nasty from the other team and performing it to his own. Turns are taken alternately down the teams.

When your turn comes, as it must, it's quite easy: read and memorize the message you have been given. Don't get in a panic if it looks impossible. Decide what category it belongs to.

Go West Young Man is a well-known phrase or saying.
Gone with the Wind is a book and a film.
Googie Withers is a proper name.
The Guildford Telephone Directory is a book.

Count the words in your message.

Decide on an approach both witty and succinct. *Googie Withers* demands something fairly obvious and decidedly down-market.

There are a certain number of what teachers call visual aids for your performance:

1. Category

a. Proper name. Thump your heart with your right hand open or closed.
b. Song. Left hand over heart, right hand towards moon, idiotic fawnlike expression on face.
c. Opera. As song, but more so.

d. Musical. As song, but the right hand then comes down to imitate chattering movement, as with glove puppet.
e. Book. Two hands together, palms up, at waist height, with little fingers touching.
f. Film. Right hand cranks an imaginary movie camera just in front and to the right of your right eye.
g. Well-known phrase or saying. First two fingers of each hand describe quotation marks about three feet apart at shoulder height.
h. Shakespeare. Mime shaking and throwing a spear.
i. Television programme. Describe a square in the air with both forefingers.

That sounds fairly simple, doesn't it?

2. Number of words

Hold up the appropriate number of fingers. You may nod, look delighted, and point at someone who has counted correctly.

3. Decide which word you are going to begin with

Hold up the appropriate number of fingers. They'll soon catch on.

4. How many syllables has it?

Bang the appropriate number of fingers on your forearm. Not, please, the forearm the fingers come on. The other one.

5. If you decide that you are going to act the whole message in one, make an encircling gesture with your arms

6. Short word: a, an, the, but, if, and . . .

Hold up an invisible thimble between thumb and forefinger and wait until one of your team stumbles on the right word.

7. Sounds like . . .

If you really find it impossible to act a syllable or word, cup a hand to an ear, wait for them to say 'sounds like', and act out a word that rhymes. Once they've got the rhyme, they'll be close to the syllable you want.

I once had to do *Quo Vadis*.

1. Film.
2. Two words.
3. First word.
4. One syllable.
5. Sounds like . . .
I imitated a bird, and my team eventually hit upon 'crow'.
6. Second word.
7. Two syllables.
8. Whole thing.
9. Sounds like . . .
I did a silent scene from *Dr Who*, and was making for the box he travels in when someone, taking pity on my shame and embarrassment, said 'Tardis'.
10. Put them together: Crow Tardis.

11. Not far to go, with a lot of ear-cupping, to *Quo Vadis*

Another example is *Absurd Person Singular*.

1. Play.
2. Three words.
3. Third word.
4. Three syllables.
5. Whole thing. Hold up one finger until someone stumbles on 'singular'.
6. At this stage a gesture indicating 'come on gang, how *many* plays do you know of with 'singular' as the third word of the title?' may be called for. If they still don't get it . . .
7. Second word.
8. Two syllables.
9. Whole thing. Point at someone and carry on pointing *emphatically* until you get 'person'.
10. As 6 until they get it right.

Now the title *Absurd Person Singular* has been given to you in the hope that you will go for the first word first, and the opposing team will be *bitterly* disappointed that you haven't. That, however, is part of the game: it's as funny to avoid making a fool of yourself as it is to do it. Sometimes. What you do is go for the trigger—the single word that will spring the whole phrase out of someone.

I like team charades because the team not guessing derives a great deal of enjoyment from deriding the other team's performances.

There are, however, other varieties.

Full team charades

The teams separate. Each decides on a word or phrase to act *as a team* and spends 15–20 minutes organising a series of playlets which will satisfactorily embody and obscure that word or phrase, first divided up into syllables and finally as a whole. No guesses are allowed from the opposition until the team has finished.

We once did *Romance*.

1. *Rome*. My father dressed up as the Pope and the rest of the team milled about being blessed. That took some time.

2. *Ants*. As *Rome*, really, except that my father took off the sheet and the teacosy and joined us.

3. *Romance*. A full B-movie scenario.

The entire performance lasted 25 minutes.

None of the rules for team charades applies to the full team version, as the main object of the latter is really to get as many people as possible dressed up in kitchen hardware.

Solo charades

Everyone, without leaving the room this time, writes out two messages and the whole bunch is put in the middle of the table. The company selects two nasties each, and everyone acts in turn. There is, on the whole, less fun in this than in being part of a team, and there is greater danger of duplication than in team charades.

TENNIS ELBOW FOOT

The name of the game indicates the rules. One person begins with a word—any word that leaps to mind—and the person on his left follows with a word connected in some way with the first one. The connexion may be synonymous, antonymous, rhyming, literary, or anything at all so long as it makes sense to the other players. This goes on round and round the table until someone falters or makes a false connexion.

A   Strong
B   Hardy
C   Tess
D   Bess
A   Black
B   White

On the face of it, there is no reason why the game should ever end. You will find that there is suddenly nothing quite as intellectually rigorous as a bunch of gamesters with their tails up enjoying this particular form of indoor croquet.

From R Harrison

ADD AN ACTION

This game needs rhythm; something simple but catchy. Two handclaps and two thumps on the table usually works well.
Thus
Clap clap thump thump clap clap thump thump . . . got that?

The actions happen during the two thumps. Once the rhythm is established, the leader begins by adding an action—say tapping one elbow with the other hand—which fits into the thump thump bit of the rhythm.

So A goes: Clap clap tap tap

Then the next player imitates the leader's action on the next thump thump, and adds another action on the following thump thump, say stamping his feet.

So B goes: Clap clap tap tap clap clap stamp stamp clap clap

The third player must come in sharp on the next thump thump, all three go back to the beginning of the sequence, and then he adds his own action.

Clap clap tap tap clap clap stamp stamp clap clap wriggle wriggle clap clap.

The fourth player then comes in, and so on round the table.

The important element is the rhythm. Don't take any nonsense from players who want to add an action on the clap and not on the thump. They'll do it on the thump and like it.

The same principle holds in a game called

Number your neighbour

Each person is assigned a number. Once a fast rhythm has been established the leader shouts out his number and then another number.

The player whose number has been shouted out repeats his own number and then another. Let's have a visual aid:

A		E		C		B	
clap	clap	thump	thump	clap	clap	thump	thump
1	5	5	3	3	2	2	ermmm

Omnes	B
You broke it!	hee haw etc.
Donkey!	
Hee hee etc.	

NAMES OF . . .

The principle of Names Of . . . is the same as that of Add an Action; players leap in turn into gaps in a fiercely beaten out rhythm.

The difference is that Names Of . . . isn't just a silly old memory test. It requires really quick thinking.

The rhythm is established
Clap clap thump thump clap clap thump thump clap clap and the first player chooses a subject.

All   clap clap
A   Names of
All   clap clap
A   FAT PEOPLE
and he provides the first one
All   clap clap
A   Sidney Greenstreet
All   clap clap
and the player on A's left leaps in with
B   Robert Morley
All   clap clap
C   Cyril Smith
All   clap clap
D   Edward the Seventh
All   clap clap
A   Tessie O'Shea
All   clap clap
B   Joshua Nkomo
All   clap clap

Failures to keep to the rhythm, hesitations and

repetitions drop out. The winner gets to choose the next category. *Not* Polish playwrights; the trick is to choose a subject that has a clear, but limited scope.

You might try colours ... London tube stations ... articles of clothing ... washing powders ... flowers ... diseases ... parts of the body ... rivers ... crimes ... beaches ... scientists ... cricketers. Anything, really.

CONSEQUENCES

Like Charades, but not like Miss Jean Brodie, the game of Consequences takes many forms.

Literary consequences

In this version of the game the players choose words at random without knowing the context into which they are going to fit.

The round leader (who may or may not be spherical, but who is the leader of the round), chooses a passage which he considers lends itself to parody. A children's book is generally successful. Say he chooses *Robin Hood and his Merrie Men*, and finds the following passage:

> In his new suit of Lincoln green, Robin strolled round the outlaw camp in the Sherwood Forest. He watched his men preparing arrows, refixing bowstrings, and carrying out sundry repairs to their weapons.

The leader has to replace certain words. It's no good choosing too many or the effect (of the expected spiked with the bizarre) won't happen. So he chooses

A colour to replace *green*
A place, to replace *Sherwood Forest*
A plural noun to replace *arrows*
A verb, present participle, to replace *refixing*
Another plural noun to replace *bowstrings*
A third plural noun to replace *weapons*.

As the rest of the group call out their choices, the leader takes them down. First he reads out the original version and then the amended one. It might have been transformed thus:

> In his new suit of Lincoln pink, Robin strolled round the outlaw camp in the Gobi Desert. He watched his men preparing Brussels sprouts, ploughing cassette tape recorders and carrying out sundry repairs to their noses.

(Even merrie men have trouble with their profiles.) It doesn't do to play many rounds, as this type of unpredictable comedy soon palls. There is not really enough challenge for the true gamester, although it is endlessly popular with children and is a palatable way of becoming familiar with the various parts of speech.

Formula consequences

Traditionally, the formula is a story with a dozen fixed elements that are chosen individually so that the unexpected provides the comedy. The story might be:

A(n) (adjective) (girl's name or occupation) met a(n) (adjective) (man's name or occupation) at (place) while (some event). He wore (what he wore), She wore (what she wore). He said to her (whatever you fancy), she said to him (more of whatever you fancy). Then he (what he did), then she (what she did),

and the consequence was (*whatever it was*).
The world said (*whatever it did say*).

Each player writes down an entry for each stage in the story, folds his paper over, and passes it on, so that the story is never presented solely through one imagination.

I don't particularly like formula consequences either, because it's too easy. My favourite is

Scrub a fairy

The players alternately draw cartoons based on captions and devise captions for cartoons.

Each player starts by drawing a little cartoon or sketch at the head of his paper and then passes it to the player on his left. A caption is put to the cartoon and the paper is then folded over to hide all but the caption, and the paper is handed on again. A cartoon is drawn to fit the caption, which is then folded over to hide all but the cartoon.

And so on, until the paper is covered on both sides. As each paper is finished it is put into the centre of the table. No-one may touch the papers until they are all complete.

The special joy of this game, unlike poetry or picture consequences, is that each element refers both ways. Each cartoon is captioned twice, each caption describes two cartoons.

The name of the game comes from a particularly joyful round played between friends. There is no clean way to describe the cartoon that led to the caption 'scrub a fairy'.

Poetry consequences

The idea is the same as in *Scrub a Fairy*. A line of poetry is chosen, say

My love is like a red, red rose

and each player heads his paper with it.

Each player then supplies his own second line, say,

And with her thorns she sits and sews

and a third as well, to begin the second couplet, say,

Poppers on my anorak

47

and then folds the paper over to show only the last line. He then passes the paper on.

The next player completes the couplet and begins a new one, folding the paper over to hide all but *his* last line before passing it on.

So on until the paper is finished.

Ingenuity is appreciated in Poetry Consequences, but although it is a testing game it lacks the wild flights of Scrub a Fairy.

Picture Consequences

The first player draws the head of an animal, folds and passes it on, the second draws the torso, and the third draws the legs. The paper is folded so that only the 'leader' lines are visible to the next player, indicating where the next section of the body should begin.

Not for sophisticates.

LAWYER

Players sit in a circle. One player at a time is the Lawyer, and you may be surprised to hear that this does not necessarily mean that he keeps the others waiting for three months and then bankrupts them.

He asks the others questions about themselves, moving round the circle quickly and at random.

But no player may answer for himself. Instead the player *on his right* answers all the questions, no matter how quick or how daft they come. The Lawyer's object is to force the player at whom he is directing the questions to react in any way.

So, B must speak for A as if he were A, answering in the first person and as truthfully as he can, searching questions about A's life, attitudes, clothes, desires, perversions etc. That 'etc' includes 'etc'. If A shows any reaction to the things B says about him, he loses and must take over the role of Lawyer. There are three ways in which the Lawyer can force a reaction:

1. He moves around the circle so fast, and in both directions, that someone eventually becomes flummoxed and answers a question aimed directly at him.
2. Players don't suppress their reactions to the surprising and slanderous things being said on their behalf.
3. Players hurriedly anticipate the surprising and slanderous things about to be said.

From C R Patmore

49

DING DONG

The players sit round a table, and one of them starts off the game by taking a fork, or some other handy solid object, in his left hand. He then turns to the person on his left and says

A   This is a Ding
B   A what? (and does his incredulity surprise you?)
A   A Ding

and on this, the fork changes hands. Player B turns to the player on *his* left

B   This is a Ding
C   A what?
B   (turning back to A) a what?
A   A Ding
B   (to C) a Ding
C   (taking fork and turning to D) this is a Ding
D   A what?
C   (to B) a what?
B   (to A) a what?
A   A Ding
B   (to C) a Ding
C   (to D) a Ding
D   (taking fork and turning to E) this is a Ding

and so on round the circle. Matchless dialogue, eh?

As if to prove that age cannot wither nor custom stale its infinite variety, A (that irrepressible funster) passes a knife around in the opposite direction, with dialogue similar in all respects to that above except that the knife is called a Dong.

Let us try to write the scene.

Ding Dong
A play in one act by Jean Ennui

The curtain rises on a dinner party, late at night. There are eight characters, named in clockwise rotation, Eh, Bee, See, Dee, Ee, Eff, Gee, and Aytch, who is dropping.

A   (to B) this is a Ding
     (offers him a fork)
     (to H) this is a Dong
     (offers him a knife)
B   A what?
H   A what?
A   (to B) a Ding
     (B takes the fork)
     (to H) a Dong
     (H takes the fork)
B   (offering C the fork) This is a Ding
H   (offering G the knife) This is a Dong
C   A what?
G   A what?
B   (to A) a what?
H   (to A) a what?
A   (to B) a Ding
     (to H) a Dong
B   (to C) a Ding (C takes the fork)
H   (to G) a Dong (G takes the knife)

Author's note: All the preceding dialogue should overlap. Rehearsals begin on Monday and we open after dessert.

51

UP JENKINS

Two teams sit opposite one another at the table. One of the teams passes a coin from hand to hand under the table.

The captain of the opposing team cries 'Up Jenkins!' when it suits him, and all the members of the team with the coin must hold both hands well above the table—the coin is of course hidden in one of the fists.

The captain then cries 'Down Jenkins!' and all the raised hands are slapped down on to the table, palms down, as hard as possible to mask the sound of the coin hitting the table.

The opponents try to locate the coin by eliminating the hands they *don't* think are hiding the coin. This is done hand by hand, and with a great deal of consultation. It is almost more fun the longer it takes because for some reason the coin takes on a significance entirely independent of its actual value.

The duel-scarred Prussian with a monocle and a cigarette holder leaned casually on the corner of the desk, a wicked half-smile playing around the corners of his mouth.

"You inhuman brute" gasped Jenkins, gingerly exploring the ruins of his teeth with a ragged tongue. "Now you'll never know where that coin has gone. Never." "Bring een zee girl" Fasser rasped curtly to Schlimmer. Jenkins could scarcely distinguish light and shade through the bloody slits that had been his eyes, but when Schlimmer

returned he saw that he could hold out no longer. With a sob he gasped to the handcuffed, gagged, trussed, blindfolded, manacled, shackled, chained girl who flew across the room and flung herself to his side.

"It's no use, mother, I'll have to tell him. Fritz . . ."

The great football of a head made the slightest gesture in his direction.

"You'll find the coin in my left hand." With a rattle and a groan Jenkins collapsed in his chair.

"Don't go to sleep, Eeeenglish, or rather, Welsh. Now it's my turn. Close your eyes while I hide ze coin. And come up here. I want to sit zere for a while . . ."

PARANOIA

Don't play this game unless you are in reasonable mental health.

One person leaves the room. The others decide on a tactic which will govern all their answers, movements, reactions when that person re-enters. He is asked to return and discover in any way he likes what the common factor is.

They might all decide to answer as if they were traffic wardens, or white slavers, or all answers might end in vowels. Or they may all decide—and this is where it becomes dangerous—that the questioner has some terrible social disease, that he has just lost his mother, or that he is deaf ...

This is a game to play to the *finish*. No quarter is given and questioning continues until either the factor or the questioner is isolated.

SALTED ALMONDS

An interpersonal manipulative strategy game. London debutantes used to play this, I'm told, with those salted almonds you can pick up for a couple of thousand dinars.

Cynthia, Amanda and Priscilla would agree upon a series of sentiments or sentences they thought they could manipulate their escorts into uttering. To show success, a deb would take a salted almond from the bowl and put it beside her place at the table. The deb with the most almonds at the end of the evening won; history isn't particular interested in the prize. The important thing was the after-dinar tot-up.

Two modern variations of Salted Almonds

Two players are each given a sentence by the rest of the company. They must not know what their opponent's sentence is. A conversation is begun, in which the two of them must participate, and which is monitored by the other players. Each of the two has to work his sentence comfortably into the talk, so that it is not spotted by his opponent. If the sentence is challenged successfully when it appears cloaked in secrecy, then the game is won by the challenger.

Hint: the company must be canny about the sentences they choose. The game isn't fun if there isn't *any* way in which the two remarks could co-exist within one conversation.

More fun may be had in manipulating one another to say or imply a predicted sentence, or action—to talk about the sun, apologise, say 'thank you', read your hand or whatever.

These games rely on nerves—and they can be field days for gamester sadists.

From C R Patmore

KILLER

I dare not fight; but I will wink ...

William Shakespeare

If this game were called Winker it would be merely diversionary. As it is it can genuinely induce fear and loathing in the third course.

It must be played to win.

A Killer is chosen—by distributing one marked scrap of paper amongst blanks, one court card amongst plain ones, etc. His identity remains, for the time being, a secret.

Conversation is continued at the nearest possible approximation to its normal pointlessness, and the Killer goes to work. His object is to wink at each player in turn without being spotted by anyone except that player. He continues to do his evil work until all the company has been winked at, or *killed*.

Each victim must wait at least thirty seconds after being killed before slumping back into his chair, on to the floor as life deserts the inanimate frame, and the others have got the idea.

The non-Killers' object is to catch the Killer in the act of winking. Anyone who believes he has seen the Killer at work must accuse the *victim* before he dies, not the Killer. If he is right, he goes on to accuse the suspected Killer. If he is wrong, then only he drops out.

Killer can be played stationary or on the move. It is most frightening when death seems to strike in the middle of normal activity—clearing the table, putting out the coffee, or whatever you do after dinner. Not that.

I have known games of Killer last for up to fifteen minutes, if the Killer himself is sufficiently patient and sadistic. The game is sometimes used as an acting exercise to heighten awareness.

HOBBY HORSE

A nifty way to reduce after a heavy meal. The company divides into two teams, which compete by carrying one another across the room.

No, do read on.

Each member of each team has to transport all his team-mates across the room one by one. The snag is that no method of carrying may be used twice by the same team. A judge is required. You should have no trouble finding volunteers.

You will find that the first methods of transportation chosen are always boring old fireman's lift, piggy back, shoulder hoist, romantic-hero toting and on the shoulders. Here are a few suggestions:

Piggyback front to front
Standing on the feet
Tucked underarm
Donkey fashion
Arms linked back to back
Standing on the shoulders (note: for those living·at Blenheim Palace *only*)
Caterpillar fashion

The Zodiac chart from Lovecraft might give you a few other ideas.

I would strongly suggest that those of you with hernias negotiate to be baggage only.

From C R Patmore

NEWSPAPER TAXIS

The Times is out of joint; O cursed spite
That ever I was born to set it right!

William Shakespeare

Equipment for this game is strictly outside the terms of reference of this book, but it is so good that I couldn't prevent it sneaking in.

Once the table is cleared, each player is given a newspaper—broadsheet size only for the best effect—which has been prepared so that all the pages are out of order.

Each player's object is to restore order in his paper. The first to do it becomes the Victor Ludicorum. No rising from the chair, no conferring, elbow and knee pads must be worn, and no, one *Observer* does not equal two *Mirrors*.

For a specially riotous evening, why not try this game without clearing away all that leftover blancmange?

From R Hartley

TRAINS

A game of surprise. One person begins by going round the table making a noise like a train. Not

Hrrrmmmm pzzzzzttt this is—er—your—um—guard speaking ppZZZZZt we apologize for the mmrrrrrmmmm mrrrrrmmmm the train—will shortly be—coming into—Rfff—will passengers please—

Not that. The noise is that of a steam engine:

PUFF puff puff puff PUFF puff puff puff

or

CHOO choo choo choo CHOO choo choo choo

He has a choice.

As he goes round, he taps someone on the shoulder and invites them to join him. They both go round

PUFF puff puff puff PUFF puff puff puff

and out of the door.

Once out of the door and beyond earshot, the surprise: A makes as if to kiss B tenderly (appropriately enough since he/she *is* the tender). At the last moment, though A *slaps* B.

B   What the hell was that for?

A   When we go in again, pick someone, we'll bring them out, I'll kiss you, you pretend to kiss them, and slap them instead. Isn't this FUN?

B   Isn't it just.

So in they go again, puffing and chooing, B picks someone, takes him out on the end of the train, A kisses B, B turns to kiss C, but slaps him instead. It is explained to him that it is now his turn to pick someone to slap after the others in the train have been kissed, and the three-part train re-enters. The process is repeated until the whole company is in the train.

It is quite good fun being part of a train if you like that sort of thing. Still, if you loathe the idea it's probably not for you.

It ought to be acknowledged that it can be depressing being the last person picked. To avoid this, bathe a lot, don't eat very much in the way of garlic or rotten eggs, smile until your teeth are dying of exposure, volunteer to make the coffee, do the washing up, DON'T talk about your job, and be at all times very matey, as in 'Hello chief/mate/guv/cocker/admiral/rear vice-marshal. My shout. What's yours?'

On the other hand, this now sounds like exactly the sort of behaviour that will get you picked last. Perhaps you should simply affect a Gallic indifference and wear tight jeans.

THE GREAZE

At Westminster School on Shrove Tuesday selected boys from each form fight a pitched battle for the largest piece of an inedible pancake flung over a twenty-foot high bar by the school chef. *Honestly*. The boy with the largest piece after three minutes is judged the winner and receives a golden sovereign from the Dean of the Abbey. This battle is known as The Greaze.

If you think that your guests are in just the mood for a spot of boisterous physical contact, chuck a handful of small eatables—nuts, mints, pork balls, dumplings—on the floor and give them three minutes.

It is possible that your guests will object to the whole enterprise, in which case I wouldn't press the topic.

FATHERS, MOTHERS AND BABIES
(The other version)

A game for large numbers of uninhibited people, divisible into groups of three. Folded slips of paper are distributed, identifying everyone as either parent or offspring of some animal. The distribution must be entirely random, and the more unusual the creature the more difficult and entertaining the game becomes.

When you receive your paper it will say something like

Mother gerbil or
Father giraffe or
Baby hippopotamus.

At a given signal, you must mill around trying to find the rest of your family by making only the noise of that animal and impersonating its movements. When the three of you are reunited the mother sits in the nearest chair with the baby on her lap and the father behind her.

The first team to do so wins, but the game must continue until every family is together, and woe to the three red-backed spiders still scuttling around at the end.

From Helen Priday

66

Bow-wow-wow

BLIND MAN'S BUFF

Surely no-one needs to have Blind Man's Buff explained to them. It goes with jelly throwing and the Oedipus myth.

However, a variation has been brought to my attention. *Two* people are blindfolded, and one is set to catch the other. The rest of the company is divided up into two teams, one shouting advice to the quarry, the other to the hunter.

The other players may find it more satisfactory to remain at the sides of the room rather than to rush about in between the blind men. In either case they are not allowed to shout advice by name.

According to whether you play the game to music, poetry or outdoors, it may also be called *Ray Charles' Buff, Milton's Buff* or *Gloucester's Buff*. Played in the nude it becomes *In the Buff*.

From C R Patmore

MURDER IN THE DARK

A number of cards, equal to the number of players, is distributed. Among the cards are the Jack of Diamonds and the Queen of Spades. Whoever receives the Queen is the Murderer and keeps it quiet; whoever receives the Jack is the Detective and tells everybody. (Folded scraps of paper, blank except for two marked D and M, will do just as well.)

All the lights in the room are turned off—although the game is sometimes played over the whole house, it's better in a single room, for reasons that will become plain. The players, Detective included, move about in the darkness, putting themselves at risk from all directions (and taking care to avoid that rather expensive vase and slightly delicate nest of tables). Everyone must make like stout Cortez and keep quiet. When the Murderer decides to make his move—and his mark—he 'murders' somebody. This must be done quite unequivocally. None of your pussyfooting about with rare untraceable poisons. The victim must be under no illusions as to the permanency of his complaint, and as he falls he must sound like a despised and dying king. 'Aaaaaaaaaaargh!' will do nicely, thank you. (It has been known for the Murderer to kill by whispering into the victim's ear 'you're dead!' We've always preferred to imitate nature.)

The Detective immediately issues two orders:

1. Don't panic.
2. Nobody moves.

In a proper game the players take no notice of either, and pandemonium breaks out until the Detective turns on a light. At this point everyone *must* freeze. The Detective is in charge.

He interrogates the company. In some circles he is permitted to interrogate the corpse as well, but even in fun a round trip to Hades is going a bit far and we don't normally allow it.

Everyone but the Murderer must answer the Detective truthfully. The Murderer can do as he likes, thereby proving his basic inability to accept any sort of social contract. It is to his advantage, though, to use as much of the truth as will support a credible alibi. The Detective has a problem in that two of the traditional lines of investigation are closed to him. There is no motive; it is the essence of motiveless malignancy. The method doesn't matter. There is only means. He must try to establish where everyone was at the time of the scream. Possible lines of enquiry that the Detective might wish to follow are

1. Question direct. Where were you at the time of the scream? (Position A for everyone)
2. Which side of you did the scream come from?
3. Is that why you are where you are now? (position B for everyone)
4. Can at least two people who were near the pathway between A and B vouch for the fact that you passed them?

71

All this will take some time, especially if there are more than half a dozen players. That's why it's better to limit movement to one room; people get bored.

The Detective is allowed two challenges. If he doesn't guess the correct identity of the Murderer, he must submit to a Forfeit.

WATERWORKS

Not strictly a game—more a mean trick, really, although there are less sophisticated moods when everyone might enjoy spraying some water around. Choose your victim with care, however, then ask him to extend both his hands, palms down, at about waist height. Two full glasses of water are then placed on the backs of his hands. He will rapidly and uncomfortably discover that it is impossible to remove the glasses without spilling the water, but the problem does diminish according to the shape and size of the glass, and whether or not the victim has metal hands.

Those whose cupboards harbour a long broomstick and a spare goldfish bowl or something similar might like to try this version. Fill the bowl with water, and find an accomplice who will hold the broomstick while you clamber on furniture to reach the ceiling, promising an astonishing spectacle. Place the bowl against the ceiling, open end up, (you will remember from Double Physics·on Friday afternoons that the water will, given the chance, fall out of the bowl). Now ask your accomplice to press the broomstick up against the base of the bowl, wedging it against the ceiling. Then climb down, and leave him there as a warning to all those toadies who volunteer to be Magician's Assistant.

MUSICAL CUSHIONS

Cushions are placed in a double row on the floor, one fewer in number than there are players.

The players stand in a rectangle around the lines of cushions, with their backs to them, and while the music is playing they must keep moving round in a clockwise direction (or anticlockwise. I'm not going to be dogmatic about it. It's a free country—though not, in this case, a free book. If you're reading this in the shop either put it back or pay for it.)

The Officer Commanding Area Cushions (who, if short-staffed, may also be Officer Commanding Area Music) removes one cushion at a time while the music is playing, so that when the music stops there is one fewer cushion than persons. Everybody dives, and those with nothing to sit on, or rather with nowhere to *put* what they sit on, drop out and the game continues until only one person remains.

The fun of the game can be increased if the OCA Cushions removes more than one each time. No point in messing about. Six people diving for two cushions is much more entertaining than for a restrained five. Also if players give no quarter *whatsoever* in obtaining a cushion for themselves.

This version of the game has several rather practical advantages over Musical Chairs. It is difficult to break a cushion, and difficult, though not impossible, to fall off one. Cushions are also softer than most chairs, and easier to move around.

SARDINES

A game for everyone who has ever wanted to say

'It's not your mind I'm interested in. It's your body. Worraworraworraworraworraworraworra...'

One person goes off and hides somewhere in the house. All games involving lights off, hiding, murdering, maiming and so on, must be played according to the house equivalents of the Geneva Convention. As in real life, it's entirely possible that no-one will stick to the rules and you may find the battle for the Ogaden going on in your garden, but that's part of the hazard of being alive.

The hider—the Ur-sardine—is given three minutes to hide while everyone else waits in one room. After three minutes the fuses are pulled, which guarantees darkness and no cheating. Bad luck on those of you with deep freezes.

The entire company spreads around the house, stealthily searching for the Ur-sardine. Everyone acts alone. When one person has found the hidden Ur-sardine he (or in this case, of course, she) hides in the same place, in as close physical contact as possible. THIS IS IMPORTANT. Otherwise you may never learn things about yourself that it would be healthier to know, and you would avoid having an awful lot of fun.

Gradually, as other searchers find the hiding place, they too snuggle up in silence (and perhaps awe) until everyone is there, packed together like—yes?—sardines. There *is* a divinity, Rough

Hugh, and this is an example.

Sardines is best played with a lot of people in conditions that prevent people being over-self-conscious. I wouldn't try it with fewer than about ten, or you won't get everything you should get out of it—crushed rib cages and divorce suits, by way of example.

DO YOU KNOW MR GREEN?

If you have the sort of parties at which people are able to recognize a straight line after nine o'clock, this one's for you.

Everybody—yes, everybody, dear—stands in a straight line. The leader, let us say for the moment the jovial and popular host, is at the head of the line and he engages the player behind him in the following Socratic exchange:

A   Do you know Mr Green?
B   No
A   He's the man who goes like this

at which A folds his arms. B then repeats the process with C, and so on down the line until all the players have their arms folded.

There are, however, few limits to Mr Green's virtuosity, for no sooner have all arms been folded than A, the President and Founder of the Mr Green Fan Club, accosts B

A   Do you know Mr Green?
B   No
A   He's the man who goes like this

at which A squats down. The question and the action are again repeated all down the line.

The entire row is now squatting, with arms folded. From the head of the queue, in a voice of thunder, comes

A   Do you know Mr Green?
B   No

(although by now you'd think he would know quite enough)

A   He's the man who goes like THIS

at which A gives B a huge push. With luck, the entire line will fall over like a row of dominoes, and everyone will laugh. Without luck they won't. This is not a game to be played twice in an evening. Or in a lifetime, really.

From Dr G D Chryssides

WHO GOES THERE?

One for the very end of a very long evening.
  One person leaves the room. The others all try to
guess who it was.